# Wiregrass Moon

# Wiregrass Moon

by

## John M. Weeks

For Irik, Jennie, and Alice

# Contents

## Wiregrass Moon

# I

# The Cold Gray Echo

## Death for Life

45 minutes until sunset;
a sharpness in the air
after four days of hard freeze.
Standing in a river bottom
all is gray and cold—still.
With airy silence between
the chirp of a rush,
or the distinct high-pitched
whine of a gray squirrel.
Always the smell of smoke
in the thin, cold air...
The swamp is still.

Its reflective black pools
fringed by duckweed,
cypress, and sweetgums.
Stone colored guards...
Their trunks as marble;
leafless branches reaching
high toward the pastel sky.
All is calm and resting—
dormant and sleeping.
The last of the sun peeks
through an exhausted canopy.
Day is coming to a close.

I see Magnolia's green leaves;
shining, waxy—contrasting.
Or the palmetto's vibrance,
like summer's chartreuse
against brown ocean carpets
of crumbling, dead foliage.
Waves and swells of leaves,
of sticks and dying things.
Rotting logs and muck, decaying
and feeding another year.
It is death for life—
soon, blooming lush and green...

For now, the river bottom rests.

## Natural War

Walking, wander to observe
the cold beach-shore scene.
Gulls, terns, and skimmers
holding fast against the
winter Atlantic's gust, wash,
and flow. See the riptide
with whitewash foam! Pushing,
receding; slowly creeping.

Leaving driftwood and shells
like remnants of some natural war.
Disorganized by constant battle
of sun, water, and roaring gusts.
Coquina dust in ripples and array
of shells. An army of seabirds.
Ruddy Turnstones huddled against
the harsh wind—the burning wind.

Brown backs and white bellies.
Darting, hopping, and sprinting,
leaving thousands of little tracks.
Royal Terns soaking warmth of sun
in view of many driftwood trees.
Crooked and angled against the
raging blue sky. Curved and half
buried in the beach desert's sand.

## Sand Dune Beach Scene

Imagine a sand dune in the winter,
Juxtaposed to murky green Atlantic sea.

With smell of salt on the air,
With steady wind rattling the sea oats.

Roots exposed, shaking in the drift.
A side view of the stratigraphy layers.

The years and years of layers... collapsing.
Timelines, some spilled out on

The rippled level. Powdery sand and traces
Of pink coquina. Wind, water— tides, wash.

Constant change is nature's commission,
As all life clings to possibilities of the sun.

## Little Ocean

Down the sugar-sand ribbon road;
a straight path to a highland lake.
A blue-green gem set and enshrouded in
scrub, lonely pines, and turkey oaks.
A first impression from above, looking
down the corridor between the scrub and
    palmettos
that lightly sweep the winter sand.

"This must be a picture of old."
Faded, stained, and washed by the sun.
Not so different from centuries past when
Timucua walked the pine barrens.
Only this washed out in memory...
All reflected in the clouds;
the big, blue-sky expanses.
Only memories and mostly forgotten.

You're inevitably drawn down to the water's
edge; a sloshing, moving translucence.
Silicon beads roll in the small waves
that have smoothed sandstones for ages.
To watch is to place your mind in a zone of
    indifference;
contrasting and separate from the reality
    beyond.
The weed line golden wheat on navy blue

Little Ocean–

It rocks and sways gently...
On the right looking out, cypress trees
stand in the shallow water as solemn guards.
They are ancient, timeless—calm.
Small fish cling to shade and hide away
under palmetto fronds that hang to the
    water.
Old dead snags tower above, pointing to the
    expansive sky.
Two eagles stand watch on towering pines.

## All While the Quiet Stillness

This river slithers its way
through limestone and sandbars
like some black serpent.
Crowned on sides with infinite
swamps and hardwood trees.
Once San Juan, now Suwannee.

Whitewashed rocks scattered;
tumbled by millennia floods.
Sharp, porous—tunneled, peculiar.
Every bend is a picture painting.
The live oak hangs to water;
crooked limb reaching—touching.

All are wrapped in resurrection ferns,
air plants, and Spanish moss.
Spattered green palmettos fringe sandy
shore, with vines suspended over
black mirror water... It seems like an
emerald, silver spring at every turn.

They bellow from the banks;
trickling and meet the black.
A contrasting line; light to dark.
Amazement! In all the little worlds
in this world, from the tops of
tree canopies, into the deep depths.
Moss covered rocks touch water's edge

above little aquatic environments below,
where crawdads and fish dart back and forth.

All while the quiet stillness…

Emersed—hearing only the lapping
of water on the side of the boat,
a Blue Jay's cry, and the subtle wind.

## Red Bellies

I went fishing on
Black Creek with
my Jennie.

For me, all of the past—
for her, something new,
all discovery.

Red Bellies love warm days in winter...
the most beautiful fish in Florida.
Planned and painted in every detail
and so very powerful alive.

We cast flashing spinners
by cypress trees and sandbars.
Feel the tick, tick, PULL!
Laugh, and reel—giggle some more.

So beautiful! Eyes drawn to
scarlet, blood red from jaw
to back fin and mid-section in
aquamarine, merging to darkest
ocean blue. Face with strands of
electric green lightning strikes.
Eye like jewel in fractured light.

We smile with her happy heart,
her busy hands and busy mind—
and questions.
All while the slow black water
making its way... still on course.
All the v-ripples and currents,
and infinite mysteries below.

Above, crooked oak canopies
and the wonders of the sun.
On a warm winter day, fishing
with my daughter on Black Creek.

## Controlled Burn

With new boots on, I walk the pinewoods;
blackened to ash and incinerated—now cold.
Slow step through the charred remains
in the aftermath of a forest fire.

No more flames—just hot spots
and a little stream of smoke
rising gently from an old stump,
just as if from a cigarette.
In some spaces all that's left is sand
or crinkly pine needles and burned up
wiregrass, black and coiled in piles
on the ground; footsteps with the sound
of crunching, glasslike pings and pops.

I imagine the rattlers and Indigos
slithering across the firebreaks
to escape the flames.
What a sight to see...
as the heavy smoke billowed,
blacked out the sun,
cleaned out, and culled the woods
of all that it didn't need.
The violence of the whole thing–
the indiscriminate aggression of nature.

Moving on slowly through remnant
strands of old growth pines;

flat topped, scaled, and wise.
Trunks fire hardened and scorched,
almost all scarred by cat faces.
Sometimes a rusty nail
that held the drains that took the pitch.
Worked by cracked, calloused hands...
tired—sore of days of hard work in the sun.
In the endless, infinite barrens,
such open spaces between the trees...
Echoes and silence—this ancient scene.

## January Prairie

Imagine a wet prairie grassland
sprinkled with palmetto hammocks.
Open, ever changing—year by year, by year.
Wind and sun, but sometimes cutting cold.

So many tribes and nations of birds:
Gallinules, Moorhens, Starlings, and ducks.
Greenback herons sitting still or stalking
with smug smiles, walking in grass mats.

All the dollarweed and cattail forests,
and aquatic fields of water hyacinths,
     yet with no bloom...
It is January—the 2nd of January.

I watch the Limpkin strutting,
speckled shoulders and breast.
Martins swooping, floating low
to high, and reckless in the sun.

White Ibis picking in the mud,
while alligators hang and drift.
They seem as sticks or logs
half submerged in the muck.

## Wood Ducks

Wood ducks are winter and dark rivers,
gunpowder smoke and steam off the water,
before fragments of sunlight break through
in the morning when the air is still and cold.

They are the spirit of the deep woods,
    shadowy and uncharted.
Just look at a drake's painted face against
    winter worlds with no color:
evergreen, purple, black, white, and gold.
Brown and speckled to blue-gray wings with
    zebra patches.

Woo-eek! woo-eek! woo-eek!
They echo against the gray trees.
Ripple on water—splashing and playing,
they whistle like a missile and surprise you.

You were there and I never saw you...
Knew of me before I knew of you...
Like an apparition ghost of the swamp.

## Sandhill Cranes

Sandhill cranes walk in lock step,
yet elegantly—majestic proud.
Prairie guards in winter morning,
red crested against white masks.
Contrary to their dusky gray-brown
or the yellow-white January grass.

They rattle-call and echo afar.
Weary and bleary on blue water,
while I rubbed my bloodshot eyes.
Wingspan and chop, chop, flap!
Ancient, Jurassic as dinosaur tribe—
Lord and great master of birds.

## A Murder of Crows

Whether in the bright sun of summer
or the cold gray echo of winter,
in reaching, leafless trees on silver skies,
a murder of crows is not hard to find.

I often see them, dark with beady eyes
and beaks picking while scheming.
Calculating a mission...
Working together, but for themselves.

Hop, jump, and glide as dots on a horizon.
Fast succession of wings flapping,
So sharp and wary, wise...
Finesse of an experienced burglar.

Sometimes the most common bird
of all around here—caws and screams!
Grabbing, stealing, Machiavellian ways;
for a frantic meal, for survival.

They read your face; know what you are up to
and they stick together, shining, jet black.
Sun reflecting on well-oiled feathers,
they fly with weary, dreary truth.

# II

# In New Shades of Green

## Redbud

Redbud crystal bloom
Pink flowers against the gray
Spring rhythms begin.

## Bees on Orange Blossoms

Bumble bees and honeybees
Make busy work on citrus blossoms.
Grabbing and curling—legs moving,
They collect powdery yellow pollen
And nectar to make honey.

Cool breeze in the morning sun
Sweet perfume of orange blooms.
Their short-lived spectacle...
By the thousands present themselves
White stars against green foliage space.

Few will make it to orange,
Yet they try in their rare moment
Unleashing a new season, a new year.
Simplicity in waving of flowers,
And innocent hum of bees.

## Red Birds

Deep blue green in early morning
Red birds sound off and repeat
with distinct anthem of spring.
Metallic chip and chirp!
And cheer-cheer-cheer...
purdy-purdy-purdy!
Ushering in the new day.

Fluttering bush to bush
in new shades of green
with azalea's plastic pink.
Brightest red flash—
flurried, electric energy.
Crested and masked;
pulling away dark curtains.
End of winter to equinox.

## Jewel of the Scrub

Sky-blue lupine—beauty in the sun,
As a capital city in the wiregrass.
Purple blue, beaded, and crystallized,
Shrouded in jade-green leaves.
Short lived jewel of the scrub
Something rare in the sandy
Wasteland barren. Only one time
In the year, yet always a wonder.

## King of the Sun

*Green Anole*

Creeping, crawling, slow
shuffle up the porch screen.
Eyes of jade; regards you
smugly. Sneak and slink—slow.
You show your strawberry throat.
Lime to brown, deliberate green;
who hides in multi-colored cloak.
Bobs his head in challenge
and hangs on ears as jewelry.
Comes out of the shadows;
A king of the sun.

## Coral Snake

Surprise!
Veiled in the matted oak leaves;
hidden under and within.
Spring and summer visitor,
startled and jump—no bite!
Black on yellow kill a fellow,
primal banded warning signs.
**Blood red**, hornet yellow,
and **black rounded nose...**
Wholly innocent and, yet
power of all oblivion within.
Frantic scurry; twists wormlike.
A moment of thought, considering
my human nature, my natural fear.
As my conscious convinced me better...
I decided it best to just let him go.

## Falling Creek

Steam rolls gently off water
underneath the sun and palm.
Trickle and current
to the still-water pond.
Duckweed and marsh grass,
while wood duck's kee.
Owl calls in distant hollow...
All in new spring aquatic scene,
hidden away past the hammock.

## Reflections

Lost in a cypress swamp,
I saw my rippled reflection
in knee deep pools of water;
my portrait in the twisted
roots, and tangled vines.
Confusion in that moment,
because the path disappeared.
Beautiful, but treacherous with
new green against the blue sky
and resonant chirps of red birds.

Cardinals singing in lonely echoes,
yet in all the serenity scene,
the swamp's tangled complexities.
My mind focused on danger...
Looking in every sunny spot
for the snakes that rarely are,
or gators below to surprise.
Convinced of misfortune like there
was surely no way out.
Yet faith and intuition did guide.

Not lost and forgotten...
a path emerged to shallower water;
to dry land and journey toward home.

## The Scrub

Remnant ridges of ancient sand dunes;
barren wasteland, long ago made the map.
Felt the cold snap wind of winter's last reach.

Here and there a crooked, lonely pine tree,
with warmth of sun radiating off rolling hills.
Warmed my bones after a cold morning walk.

Myrtle oaks and little clumps of palmettos;
the ground covered in lichens and deer moss.
Many heaps of little sticks washed together

by torrents, where volleys of raindrops made
impressions in sand under rusty sagebrush.
A cratered waste, just like the moon's surface

I heard the lonely question call of a bobwhite
    quail, yet I never saw a scrub jay.
Maybe I never will..., but the sound of the
    quail was good enough.
The sun's warmth, after a cold morning walk,
    was even more.

## King Bird

Red Shouldered hawk
that killed my chickens
scouts and patrols
every part of the yard.

Sitting on the fencepost,
Barred chest and checkered wings
with hues of red, black, and white.
Sharpness in all features.

King Bird

Eyes, beak, talons, tail;
gliding silent through the oaks.
Spread wings carry his body
like a torpedo on target.

Catches the black snake,
catches the mouse, and the squirrel.
Hop and stomp, rip, and tear—
All void of any emotion.

King Bird

## Spanish Moss

Someone told me that Spanish moss
came here by way of the Spanish,
    but that wasn't true.
That Timucuan women wore it as skirts...
I still wonder if that was true.
I always pondered the red bugs,
but then someone told me that Spanish
moss doesn't carry red bugs, and that's
    only a myth.

I don't really know, but I remember the
moss-man monster at the park, red eyed and
    scary to the little kids at Christmas.
I've seen it hanging from crooked
    oak limbs in full moon light.
In the thirties they used to gather it
    and sell it to make rope.
The inner black fibers are quite strong.

It makes a mess in my yard and gets tangled
    in the weed eater,
but it sways so gently in the afternoon;
    in the breeze coming off the lake.
Hangs solemn across the ages to tell
    so many stories.
Their eyes saw it, just like my eyes see it.

## Turkey Hunt

Walked the woods for three days
in cold mornings and hot afternoons.
Shrouded in spring's full foliage
against pale-blue jet stream sky.
We follow tracks in hot, dry sand.
Thirsty and tired; yet replenished by
shade of swamps and oak hammocks.
Considered impossibilities of pine rows,
flat with bottlebrush and palmettos,
yet appreciated the struggle and search,
because that is all it is, and all we have.

Each morning new gobbles and hang ups
with crows and cardinals to confuse.
In the world of the wren's low brush home...
Into this world to see as they see
and to blend and be as they are,
with insects and snakes and all of life.
Buzzing and moving warm and cold,
before the sun, in the sun, and after the sun.
All with whispering conversations; wonders,
curses, and quiet laughs.
With a last-ditch effort, a ghost apparition
bird's crackling gobble in the distance,
    in the burn in late morning.

Sends us scrambling for cover,
like under fire to crouch and duck.
And so quickly he comes closer.
Ironic that it could be this easy...
after how we've struggled and time spent.
Closer and closer, looking ahead
to enter the killing field with gobble
and drum as if vibrating the ground.
In disbelief I would see that this animal
    even exists.

Yet emerging from the high brush,
a deity of the sun in golden to copper tones;
blues and greens—unbelievable in full strut!
As if floating like a balloon across the
    wiregrass, open ground.
Tail feathers fanned and barred, rust to black
Head like lightbulb with red, blue, and white.
No concern other than here and now...
Raw instinct as a creature normally cautious,
to walk, almost willingly, into oblivion.

## Vines

Out of the wastes of cold winters,
vines come creeping and crawl
wherever they are allowed
and not allowed—trespassers.
Enshrouding, wrapping everything
and blocking the needed sunlight.

Wild muscadines, Poison ivy,
creepers, and Greenbriers
overtake with blankets and veil,
crawling into every crevice.
Wrapping trees and eventually
shaded darkness—suffocating.

Yet vibrant green where nothing
else can prosper, with reaching
growth and shining, waxy leaves.
As the nature of something that
wants to win so badly... something
that will, if allowed, and left alone.

Creating a symbiotic, parasitic lull;
perceived beauty, from distance,
though marked by strife and struggle.
You must burn the links, pull the roots,
and dig the bulbs, allowing true potential
of trees illuminated in sun's new light.
Life exposed as what is meant to be;

no longer held and constricting,
with branches reaching full measure.
Finding warm days and new days
as sun will reach to the forest floor...
Freedom of movement, heart, and mind.

## St. John's River

St. Johns slinking, slowly moving north
as murky tea-water beyond cypress trees,
while eelgrass beds lay, wave, and sway.
And clusters of arrow root and cattails
hold alone in shallows far beyond the bank.

Mullet jumps and splashes, giving surprise—
Kaploosh!

as high tide brack water reaches on top
of sandy banks covered in cypress knees.
Out across the river from Picolata,
the sun's blaze and clouds form
for future thunderstorm cycles...
Whitewashed—burned in history
as certain summer settles in.

## Atamasco Lily

Atamasco Lilies, after first spring rain
Pop and sprout in swampy meadows and
    riverine terrain.
As shining stars, new year to come
Resting in light from sun above
Gives subtle charm off beaten paths
What little time this flower has...
But rest assured next year's return
After winter's cold and season's whirl
The white rain lily, beauty profound
Returns from hiding in the ground.

## Santa Fe River

Birthed and cradled, the Santa Fe River
emerges from the lake of its name...
Out into the swamp—stagnant like a ditch,
slowly taking form through pine forests,
through the bogs and dark unknown places.
Long until a proper river begins to grow,
crawling and trickling, it slithers and flows.
Clay bottoms hold water causing floods;
as decaying leaves and vegetation stain
the water a dark color, like dirty motor oil.

Pressing on, it flows west into the plains,
then drains through porous sand and rock.
Into subterranean worlds; darkness realm.
Disappears—returns again and again.
This time with springs that clear the water,
adding strands of emerald greens and blues.
Creating contrasts of light and dark
Land shaped and formed by the
        relentlessness of water...
Eroding limestone and bedrock—karst.

All the while, in my small fragment of time;
juxtaposed to the river's infinite age...
I sit in the morning while my girls play,
considering all of Santa Fe at end of spring.
Crawling quietly through sunlit morning
        and new leaf green...

Dark water ripples over limestone rocks
behind cypress trunks and cypress stumps,
while little bream glide in the sunny spaces.
A river that starts as nothing and becomes
    something,
yet cares little for time, or turning back...

## River Oaks

Drove down State Road 13 to write
about the St. Johns River flowing north...
Taken by river oaks guarding the banks
in their far reach and stretch for light.
Clothed in resurrection ferns and air plants;
holding Spanish moss, loose in river breeze.

Limbs curving, overlapping in curious ways...
gives visions of ocean waves and stormy seas.
Same curved limbs were chopped and cut
by 'Live Oakers'; used for L bracing in ships
that sailed the world and fought many wars.
Heavy, thick limbs—fibers twisted and strong
like iron against cannonballs, or trials
    of the sea.

"If old trees could talk", so often spoken...
To see changes of the river scene; storms and
seasons, and footprints here—now vanished.
The hundreds of journeys around the sun...
These Live Oaks, trunks rooted—strong.
Gifts of the material world that connect us to
    lost ages.

## Gopher Tortoise

In bright light of mid-afternoon,
I saw a gopher tortoise make its way
through crunching leaves and wiregrass,
while prickly pears bloomed in yellow,
and a butterfly landed on orange milkweed.

Saw a gopher tortoise make its way...
Living between present and all of the past;
chomping grass and bulldozing through.
Leaving tracks and slide marks in sand,
his mind directed by reptilian blueprint.

Living between present and all of the past;
all gopher tortoises are ancient in spirit...
Millions of years, adapted—evolved
to live in sand, under pines and blackjacks.
Scaled, paddle feet—shell smeared with clay.

All gopher tortoises are ancient in spirit.
Skeptical, with habits and cautious word...
Black beady eyes; mouth caked in chlorophyll
Moving quickly to a sand aproned burrow,
sliding out of sight into a subterranean home.

## Rattlesnakes

Rattlesnakes are burning hot electricity.
Buzzing danger; warnings with banded faces.
When I was ten, just one step from disaster
in a blackberry patch. No rattle and coiled
      at ready,
yet decided not to strike, choosing to vanish.

Rattlesnakes make us consider our mortality.
Intuitions tell us to run away fast,
yet we stay—can't take our eyes from them.
Hypnotic and primal, brings reckoning...
At least we grant respect for their beauty.

With intricate patterns as perfect collage,
mirroring everything in the landscape.
The angular lines, yellows, browns, whites.
Ghost apparition vanishing in the palmettos.
Often present—most of the time unknown.

## The Ancient Sand Dune Trail

Ancient sand dune trail—not what one would
expect.

Once the edge of the sea a thousand years
    ago...

Now covered with lush forest: Live Oaks,
    palmetto, and cedar.

The sun's evolving–fractured light breaks
    through the canopy.

'The light is sweet, and it pleases the eyes to
    see the sun.'

## Netted Pawpaw

Netted Pawpaw in the forest
Golden yellow, April's bloom
Humble flower, sandy soil
Vibrant green leaf, summer soon.

They won't last as long as wanting
Upland sun, its brightest rays
But a blessing in this flower
Faithful marker, season's change.

## Full Moon Tonight

There's a full moon tonight
and the whippoorwills are going
like they do at the end of spring,
right before the real heat sets in.

The windows are open to let in the cool...
there is low talking in the background
coming from inside the house.

With late spring rhythms of night—
the newness that is ending,
yet the potential of summer unfolds.

Crickets are singing in full chorus;
buzzing energy, yet peaceful and cool.

The quiet and calm—
my thoughts wander...
-reference point-

As silhouetted outline of crooked oak limb
holds strong, and silver lining clouds
intermittently screen the moon rays...
Fluctuating as coming and passing of
    thoughts.

# III

## Sun Evolving—Fractured Light

## Blackberries

Paddled my canoe three quarters of a mile,
to get out and walk three quarters of a mile
in the lake marsh... making my way
    to the blackberry patch.
Hot, humid with thunderheads on horizon;
at first notice, black dots obscured by
    distance.

A closer look—black glowing berries
at peak for picking... watching for snakes.
Blackberries are give and take—sacrifice.
Just as Plath became a reluctant blood sister,
stickers are wincing and necessary reality.

Where my hands go, I watch.
In a sea of thorn bushes;
berries green, to red, to black.
Or white flower scene sets memory...
Always a slight feeling uneasy—cautious.

Remembering paintings of upland farms,
fixed above my grandmother's couch.
Enshrouded by thorns and thistles...
Envision sandy soil, while a cottontail skips.
Its passageways linking sections of the patch.

After a while, my bag three quarters full,
I make my way back through tall grass.
Fingers stained in splotches of purple,
while warm breeze blows over the new
     green leaves.
Watching a last quarter moon—illuminating;
my purpose here, this day complete...
On to new beginnings, I find my way home.

## In the Spatterdock Lilies

*Largemouth Bass*

Out in the spatterdock lilies,
fishing for the fish that hunts...
Against walls of elephant grass;
they lurk in dark corners of growth.

Muddy smell of summer water
with ripple and subtle breeze,
in closing moments of daylight...
Popping heat-lightning while ducks fly,
canoe's gliding course by the wind.

Cast, flip, bounce on muddy bottom,
like crawdad, worm, or minnow.
Tick, tick, heavy, dead weight,
as pulling against a sunken tire,

yet roll and swirl—flashing roll.
Jumping, shaking, what a wonderful fish!
Large open mouth with ruby gill plate.
To grab with thumb and pointer finger...
clench, admire, and behold!

Array of colors—camouflage collage,
Dark muddy greens, lateral line in black;
perfectly created to lurk, and ambush
out of grass, from behind the snags.

Quick flashes and strikes to shock
the minnows, shiners, crawfish, and frogs.
Aquatic world, murky... sun shining through.
Bubbles, wind currents, and swimming fins,
I lower him back to the underwater realm.

## Our Part of the River

This is from my memory–
Magnolias over black water,
White blooms, tender and new,
Floating slowly with tide currents
Where forests melted into water.

We were young and I ungrateful,
Though I saw the beauty in this
and I saw such beauty in you.
We jumped into cool, cleansing water
Just beyond the railroad bridge.

Our part of the river...
Hanging limbs, lilies, and all
Your sun smile and auburn hair
As we lay in the sand laughing,
With summer's green and cicada's song.

## Harvesters

*Florida Harvester Ants*

Florida harvesters trickle in and out;
their apron bed ringed with silica
and charcoal from the burn.

Rusty red fire, some bull headed
with mandibles and stinger poison...
Learned as a child—clenched my teeth.

Hard they labor as example,
placing seeds in granaries
in subterranean tunnels below.

Making most of xeric landscape—
desert scape and sandy soil,
for queen, colony, and common goal.

## Six Lined Racerunner

Along the barbed wire fence
on hot sand and sunlight glow,
startled by quick zip and rustle—
rattle of the oak leaf piles that
enshroud the white ribbon road.
Thought it a snake, but just
    a racerunner.

Six lines—some golden stipes
to contrast the black and blue.
Darting, zipping into wiregrass
patches and then out again.
Stand, watch; would never catch,
and some things I'd never try.

## Palmettos

*Inspired by 'Shadows on the Sand' by Zonira Hunter Tolles*

Saw palmettos clumped and still,
held within the live oak shade.
Sun evolving—fractured light,
wild grape vine gently hangs.

Passing 'Shadows on the Sand,'
Landscape's story to conceal.
Past in shrouded mystery
Green palmettos forming veil.

## Little Bats

Little bats, flicker flap,
short glide, swoop!
Fading sky, tree line,
as the day is through.

Cicada, cricket chirp, chirp;
flitter, flutter round...
Moth, mosquitos in the night,
they hunt without a sound.

## Arrowheads

In hot open spaces,
In the washed-out rain gullies,
We used to look for arrowheads
In mud, clay, and trickle water.
Or pockmarked sand stretches;
Searching for lost remnants.

Hours walking, talking—barefoot.
You would follow lightly behind,
Broken ground, exposed layer lines.
Must've been an ancient village;
Chert flakes and pottery shards,
Coral and rippled serrated edges.

Eye's focus for the pointed edges
Sticking out from clay-tinged sand,
Or maybe simply laying out flat.
Washed away from the ageless layers;
Beige or white and catching eye,
Out in the open field, one mile in.

I really had no fear with you,
I guess I never dug too deep.
Searching places already disturbed
In summer heat with approaching storms.
The land remembers our barefoot trails,
Yet they too have washed into memory.

## Alligators

Alligators resting, nesting in the prairie
    marsh.
Saw one segmented, cracked—slate skinned,
Bristled tail, sitting still, lurking, always
    watching.

Dragon-like bellow, while bullfrogs croak,
Red-winged Starlings nervously buzz around.
Monstrous head and pale, baggy throat
    raised high.

Protecting grass heap nests and dinosaur
    eggs,
in little pools amongst cattails where the drag
    marks are.
Rustle of reeds with warnings to stay away.

Sometimes hanging in open water, thinking
simple, primal thoughts—contemplates the
    next move,
cruising like silent ships with little wakes.

Several laying up on the muddy banks
    soaking the sun,
as herons and egrets walk by with lack of
    concern.

## Black-eyed Susan

Black-eyed Susan's simple beauty,
In the fields along the fence wire.

Yellow, golden, sunburst rays,
Shining happily from sandhill soil.

With hopeful eyes standing strong and tall,
Respite from heat and summer rain.

## The Resting Pool

Hidden away—an offshoot trail,
down into the ancient cut.
Opening to tropical oasis world;
damselflies guiding the way
in black and neon-green or blue,
while sounds of water rushing;
trickle, splash, and sloosh.
Little falls of cool water,
emerald-blue translucence,
into pools where bay roots reach.
Away from the concentrated sun
of the wiregrass land above.

Sandy stream snakes its way,
winding—coiling into little baths.
Sit and crouch on bank to watch
as small minnows dart and play.
Light breaking canopy shade above,
illuminating spider webs or dew drops;
highlights the bright green of ferns,
driftwood resting, palmettos arch.
Collision and mixture of many things
held together at the resting pool,
while leaf boats float the rapids
around the corner and out of view.

## River Dock

Water lapping against weather worn pilings...
This I know so well, as anyone who knows
    the river.
Brackish water, murky brown with the smell
    of boat's exhaust,
it's passengers drinking beer and wearing
    sunglasses.

By now intense as the mid-afternoon–white-
    hot heat.
Two boys run and jump off the end of the
    dock;
cursing, splashing and laughing like they do.
Jumping—scurrying back up the dock to do it
    again.

Just like the blue crab below scurries over
    riprap,
patterned like shades of sky down it's claws
    and legs.
Many river fish and the prospects of
    shellcrackers and bass—
Myriads of fish you can't see, yet faith says
    they are there.

And all the while looking up the bank at
    those that dawdle
in the shade and shadows, in the grass near
    crooked trunks.
Picnicking and smoking—chatting and
    passing time;
smell of tobacco on air under oaks and
    ash trees.
It's not long before I decide to move on and
    travel north, down river.

**Lake Santa Fe**

Eyes to the shore and the grandfather cypress
trees...
All cloaked with moss and feathery green.

Ancient bulbed trunks—gray with many
    faces...
living in deep water, hollowed and tunneled.

The shore doesn't end, just fades into the
    swamp...
where echoes of frogs and birds color the air.

## Wiregrass Moon

Last of the sun went down
over rolling new-green hills,
within the scattered pines and cat faces;
tepid breeze and mockingbird's last song—

Cicadas fade and crickets chirp,
while Chuck Whippoorwill swoops;
frog song and revelation—a full moon
showing sandy ribbon, reflection trails.

The turning I felt, at the halfway mark...
Material markers that connect to the past;
wandered in dark, yet in light of moon
with splintered, refracted light over the lake's
    glassy water.

A phosphorus light, a wiregrass moon...
Quiet still—pine branch and first stars,
where we walked imagining old worlds,
where we could just be as we are.

In moonlight grass and blackjack shadows,
lost behind clouds then shown again,
pulling like tides that turned—eb and flow.
A time and place, while we lived as seers.

## The Headsprings

Heart racing plunge into the headsprings,
to glide over open silver-blue caverns.
just as a plane passing from high above
with water chilling to the core—numbing.

Catching breath at the surface in warm air;
cicadas, so loud to muffle the chitter-chatter.
The circulation swirl pushes you away;
forces you to explore the edges of the
    emerald pool.

In eel grass, duckweed—amongst the sticks
and logs, and sun reflections on silver specks.
Turtles paddle-crawl and crawfish open claw,
where fish hang, looking on cautiously.

Stumpknockers, Bluegill and bass,
all detailed in such specific clarity;
spots and speckles, and dark lateral lines.
Fins and eyes suspended in luminous blue.

Watching an intruder into their world—
Beauty overwhelming, hidden in plain sight.
Amazed as water spills over into the stream,
taking new life—rushing ahead with new
    purpose.

## Banana Spider

Banana Spider;
white capped
snowy head.
Predator's face,
geometrically dotted
abdomen with
fuzzy legs.

Hangs in shady
places where
fractal light
covers ground.
Black and yellow-
golden appendages
suspended on the trail.

Sticky yellow
spider web
startled, yet
so harmless.
All while distant
voice of stream's
trickling water.

## Little Ocean, Part II

This time I see from the water looking out...
Gentle rise of the topography in distance,
the thin ribbon-road making its way up
through twisted, tangled limbs and
    palmettos.

Far beyond, looking at the scrub ahead
where a fine line of fog hangs in early
    morning;
quail song in distance with slow wind.
It's summer now and my outlook different,
June's sun beginning to blaze overhead
and the air is very heavy already at 8 a.m.
No wheat weed line, but green and vibrant,
yet the water appears jade—still a jewel.
Moving toward the tower, where bluegills
    bed.

Schools of bass carrying on in summer ways,
flipping and flopping and chasing shad in
    open expanses.
We used to catch millions when we were free;
my bare feet hanging in the water and mind
    uncontained.
Tepid water so warm even in early hours...
Surface like a solar panel in the scrub sun,
taking on a similar structure, but never the
same.

Little ocean...

Looking in now as the bay trees are in bloom,
where the creek pushes the sandbar far into
    the lake,
where the snag makes home for the Ospreys
and the reeds gently rustle in summer and
    winter wind.
The cypress still a solemn guard—calm and
    ageless...
Similar rhythms, but never exactly the same.
Only reference of memory as boat slides
    through water.

## Bluegill

Down in murky blue water;
pockmarked sand nests
among deadwood sticks
and green grass edges.
Bluegill bed and suspend
in clumps by hundreds,
chasing golden hooks
and woven nightcrawlers
that trail through the sand.
Sporadic tick-tick-tap-tap,
their heavy fight and haul.

Blending of colors mimicking
the environs where they live;
purple headed and full grown—
bronze and gold to black ear,
mid-center pale blues and red fins.
Vertical lines breaking pattern
to conceal from many predators
below surface of open water.
Flip and flop and spine me...
Slippery to the damn catch!
Yet worthwhile, as eyes admire.

## Morning Drive in June

Morning drive—passing time in June
Saw patchwork farms, pastures, and pine
    rows,
all scattered with flowers in purple, yellow,
    and white.
Open fields—cows and distant oak tree walls,
desolation of clearcuts, burns, and mounded
    earth,
Yet little black streams and cypress heads,
where natural meets the work of man—
    dichotomy and collision.

**Heatwave**
When the real heat sets in
you will know—no question.
Misty, hazy, and white on horizon,
reflects off water as if to boil.
It enshrouds and hugs you,
dense—sweating a constant state.

I've felt as if crazy,
as heat creates a sickness
in the stomach and in the mind.
Only hope of evening and morning
cool to look forward to.
Oppressive—and we long for rain.

Hottest month, a Florida July;
even the cicada struggles to speak...
Birds flicker slowly—play in baths
and shake the water to cool,
while the lake is still and silent
with reflections of sun-bleached clouds.

## On the Edge of a Thunderstorm

First you hear a rumble in the west,
and nervous clouds begin to form.
Pulling—creating a vacuum...
like oxygen is sucked from the air,
and heavy tropical heat settles.

On the horizon, darkest clouds;
colors like gray to navy blue.
Enveloping thunderhead skies
with smell of water—drop by drop
a quiet stillness comes over.

Anticipation of cool, cleansing rains...
A sprinkle, then sparse bullet drops,
while tree frogs cheer them on;
pop, crack, electric flash and rumble!
So fast you would never know your death...

Yet the worst will pass by on the edge;
to the north the distant clouds—
They tower and you can see the rain
hanging like veils touching to the ground
as sunlight breaks through in heavenly rays.

## After the Rain

After the rain, the cooling down...
Frogs in the marsh, in the lake come alive.
Chirps and groans, croaks and honks,
Leopard frogs in front, the tree frogs behind.

Summer sounds with waxing crescent moon,
and heat lightning pops in distant clouds
behind last thunderheads of the weary day;
static, sporadic light show as if in battle.

Mosquito's whining hum and hover
Humid cool as rain drops fall off trees above.
Stars shine amongst broken clouds...
mind floating with the steady breeze.

## Welcome Visitor

Ruby throated hummingbird,
wild eyed and precision flight.

Brightest red and emerald green;
color for the gloomy, rainy day.

Through my window watching,
hovering, zipping and dancing.

Stretching—reaching gardenia flowers;
dart, dart to the hanging feeder,

in plastic red with yellow flowers.
Welcome visitor in rainy summer gloom.

## Cottonmouth

Of all creation I love,
they frighten the most—
unnerve me, yet draw me
in, like Kaa's spell…

Coiled in waiting places
with Zorro mask—ripple
scaled with bull's eye marks
of black, brown, and green.

Slow slither, then scurry
through swamp shade;
the sun and the mud
or murky water—searching.

Under turned over boats,
amongst the cypress knees.
Piled out on the sand;
watch your step!

Death in his mouth
and "daggers in his smile."
A heavy weight to be hated–
to be fated as a Cottonmouth.

## Halfway Around the Sun

It is midday now;
a harsh warmth is rising
after four days of heavy heat.
Halfway around the sun...
standing in the river bottom,
all is bright and green.

Frog song and jay's call,
or cicada rhythms,
and mosquito's whine.
Stagnant smell of swamp;
remaining reverent,
yet not so still as winter.

Black pools are covered
over by knee high arrowroot.
Cypress and sweetgum
pillars still rise, standing, guard—
reaching high with full foliage,
creating a light green canopy.

Blocks the hazy sun-sky;
buzzing, liquid energy,
Vibrant, moving, living.
It seems there is no end
to the sun in summer.
Magnolia still set apart...

Its green waxy leaves with—
grandeur of blooming white flowers.
Moss covered logs—viridescent carpet,
and the palmetto's sharp finger vibrance
over the hidden ocean of dead foliage;
the waves and swells still there.

The sticks and dying things
that fed and fueled life,
gave life from death...
Halfway around the sun—
blooming, lush, and green.

## Pilgrimage

My yearly visit for the Striper run is
is a homecoming—a pilgrimage.
I hear and remember
the oldest familiar sounds;
bullfrog's croak in the floodplain,
the deep, dark, hollow edges
of a black, stained, sandy creek.
And everything lush in summer green
It is the last day of June;
truly hot under blazing sun

Yet the river rests in coolness,
in the early morning hours.
I search for silver ocean fish,
trolling fake plastic minnows;
wobbling, rattling, shiny lures:
chartreuse, fire-tiger, or white on red.
Stripers should be here in swarms,
to spawn and lay eggs in secret spaces
of cold, canopied water, or deep holes
over sand, limestone, and gravel beds.

Boat moving through time,
V-ripple on the water— upstream,
passing others with no news or bite...
conjecturing in country voices and
    sunglasses,
yet all my efforts bring nothing.

No violent, shocking, strike and pull,
no scuffle, scurry, frantic fight,
or flopping, shining, black-lined fish.
Maybe because the world is heating up…
I decide to just settle for the scene—

And watch Gar roll, breaking mirror water.
Remember shadowy darkness of floodplains,
cicada fire and sawtooth hickory.
The sharpness of the ravine's million-year cut
and all the trickle springs and streams,
with moss covered limestone gravel,
while dragonflies dance and skim the black…
and gators slink into water around bends.
Never seeing them, just little ripple waves.
All the reasons why—my yearly pilgrimage.

## Fossils

Searchers of dark hidden places—distant off
　　the path;
through stratum of the limestone and gravel
　　beds,
or the gray gumbo clay, and stinking mud.

Walking in spilling streams as explorers
　　under palmettos and oaks;
mosquitos buzzing while snakes slither
　　through tannic water.
Re-creating the imagery—reconstructing lost
　　ages.

Where fossils lie and you would never know...
Where Mammoths, Mastodons, horses, and
　　camels gathered,
all of them around limestone sinks like an
　　African savannah.

Pleistocene and Holocene—long before we
　　arrived
with spears and tools and culture; to hunt
　　and track,
or longer before that, the aquatic marine
　　worlds...

where mighty Megalodons roamed blue
oceans,
snatching and tearing with massive, sharp
teeth.
Now digging, screening—shaking away the
sand and mud.

Hoping... mostly finding nothing, yet
sometimes thunderbolts!
Revelations—evidence of the Jurassic or the
ice age worlds before us.
Now in the subtropical—Florida with
palmettos and oaks.

Now bones and teeth... once living, dying,
decaying;
by chance, leaving remnants as a record and
reference.
Their places in time—eons and eras
unimaginable.

## Waxing Gibbous (Night Fishing)

Night fishing at summer's midpoint
under white waxing gibbous moon;
two brothers whisper, talk—philosophize,
while drone and murmur of night settles.

Praise! For the sun is sleeping...
Let the bats swarm and flicker
as they do in night sky over tepid water,
while water laps and washes on aluminum.

Weary-watching early Fourth fireworks;
spark-pop! on distant, dark beaches.
Hear the cast, buzz-plop of plastic frogs,
and low hum of Skydog's slide guitar.

We move through the generations of night—
through countless ages of a long friendship.
To unravel secrets and complete the puzzle...
to pull meaning in light of the gibbous moon.

## Mosquitoes

Zeeeeeeeee,
zeeeeeeeee,
zeeeeeeeee,
zee-slap!

## Wild Muscadines

Raindrops glimmer
on many muscadines
after cleansing
summer rain.
Enshrouded in
Cicada's song—
Speckled leaves
and twisted vines.

Peak of solstice...
three quarters
of the way
around the sun.
I break the skin,
the lifeblood sweet
and tart—wincing,
yet sensing renewal.

Nourished... nurtured
by summer sun,
and gives way to
joy in change.
Discovering new
beginnings—
journey toward
fall equinox.

**Herping**

We go because we have to make our own fun;
    all our ways to fight the boredom.
Explore hot summer roads as the sun dies—
yellow-lined and dark with uncut grass walls.

High moon—we drive watching and waiting
    for slithering snakes crossing the roads.
Yellow rats, water snakes, and arrays of frogs.
With cautious stop and walk in headlight
    glare;

flashlights floating, bouncing—quickly halt!
The scary water moccasin coiled with pale
    face pointed high,
and our nervous laughing while keeping
    distance.

They all run back to the car, to search again—
moving forward through distance and time;
our car passing through the patchwork pine
    rows and farmland.

## Bear Tracks

Evidence!
Impressed in the rain-marked sand,
pads, toes, claws—so many tracks,
crossed behind as I was not looking.

Didn't see the Black Bear moving
through the scrubby brush like a ghost;
dark, shiny coat like midnight coal.
Bulldozing through the palmettos,

or clawing and peeling cypress trees.
Seeming, rare and hardly ever seen,
yet did see them once—lumbering
across that open grass meadow.

Heart rate as beating drum, but no
harm done; watching, worried
and amazed as they disappeared—
disintegrated into the wooded wall.

## The Clearcut

In August's morning sun, began a journey
to search gray, windswept clearcuts.
Scrub-oak hammocks off on the horizon,
while determined blazing orb rose in the east.
Sweat on brow—press on into barren land;
the sandy road's gentle rise and fall ahead.

Wastes of the barren hellscape out ahead—
bright sun questioning my journey.
The sand pine skeleton piles upon the land;
left burning—scorching, endless clearcut.
My direction north, a tree line to the east;
land-swells and hidden ponds on horizon.

Pedaling hard. closer hammocks on horizon;
road rising, falling like a ribbon in the wind.
Checking the woodline wall in the east;
sweat-soaked and tired by the journey.
Man-made hellscape—all of the clearcut;
for this was once beautiful, forested land.

Once sand pines covered this rolling land;
you could never see the far, sunny horizon.
All the deer trails before endless clearcut—
They could not see so far out ahead...
I wonder if I will see a bear on this journey
into the dark green wood wall to the east.

Shadows roll—sun higher now in the east;
all of the many tracks upon this open land.
Tracks of turkeys and deer on this journey,
hammock ahead and secret pond on horizon.
Crossing over to forest in the shade ahead;
there's no way to rest in heat of the clearcut.

Look from the hammock, out to the clearcut;
dark and mysterious woodline to the east.
I turned around—gentle expanse of a pond;
birds and all life cling to this stretch of land.
Focus on here and now, not wasted horizon...
Nor on the difficulty of the tiresome journey.

The blazing clearcut—scar on the land
The woodline to the east... eyes to horizon
Rolling hills ahead, where I began a journey.

## Aquifer

Down in the caverns,
in the limestone pores,
lie sustaining waters,
crystal blue and clear.

Replenishing through
all the multitude taps;
the wells we drill
into layered lime rock.

Pumping the water
for bellowing fountains;
artesian wellspring
from subterranean lakes.

Exposed in blue-green
gem springs—jade.
Always cold when summer
heat will not give.

Spilling 26,000 year
old glasses of water–
filling my cup
when I am thirsty.

## Zebra Longwing

Zebra Longwing floating by,
Breezy day, and summer's sigh.
Black wing, white, and red dot too,
Unfolding veil of afternoon.

# IV

# Earth's Tilt Makes Shadows Long

## Hurricane

Hurricane brings
tropic wind
and <u>end</u>
to summer,
pushing—shoving
the bendy trees,
I stand lock kneed.

Power gusts
and parallel moss
as pines move.
Violent thrash!
God save the
powerlines...
I watch lily pads
flip and flap.

Wind sucks
the breath
from my nervous
lungs with
white capped water,
and torpedo birds
amongst the
zipping clouds.

## Blue-Winged Teal

When the Teal come in
we are set for change.
Summer makes last stand;
hot, heavy, and muggy,
yet cool tinge breeze.

We paddle weed choked
marshes, amongst the
reeds and spatterdock,
to see swirling flocks
of Blue-winged Teal.

Rolling like jets in formation,
Seeming white from afar—
blue flash wing patch,
come closer, like crisp
sky to usher in autumn.

Sounding like rushing wind...
passing, swooping, circling,
acrobatic and up again.
Slowly rising above tree line
and fading far, then gone.

## Shrimping

In early September we walk
down a shadowy, dark river dock;
rising pale moon and moving tide.
Ripple on water and current's flow,
we throw the bait and set our lights—
rest easy, unfolding weighted nets.

Mind wandering—pondering this tradition.
Thinking of the platforms in the sholes
where old-timers floated inner tubes
with wash buckets full of ice and beer.
They'd drink and talk and throw the nets—
gas lanterns hanging in haloed light.

Mind returning and first swinging cast,
half opening and half hopeful, yet nothing.
Though, second and third try—
we see the eyes reflecting red
and beady as we shake the net.
The old familiar sound along
the river, like muffled hammering;
echoing through murky, stagnant air.

Many little shrimp drop in fetal form,
colored blue-green of the ocean floor.
Black tip tails flicker-scratch the dock boards,
as children pick them up by antennae feelers
while smiling bright...and little croakers flip-
flop on planks before we throw them home.

## Long Shadows

As summer's gradual nearing end,
Earth's tilt makes shadows long.
Bringing on lighter air,
Mourning dove, a solemn song.

Fall flowers begin to bloom,
Blazing star and Susan's eye.
Slowly walk the wiregrass,
Summer solstice, waning sigh.

## Acorn Drop

I hear the ping and pop
of acorns drop on the
tin roof garage next door.

And rustling branches as
squirrels pick–jumping
from limb to limb.

Some sit nervously munching,
watching as I watch them
eating yellow acorn innards.

In the overcast autumn breeze,
Live Oaks become feed trees
and echoes carry differently.

All while crow call in distance,
smoky scent and hue—tinged gray;
a drizzling rain crosses the pond.

On they ping and pop—drop,
rolling to litter the ground
from crooked limb over sandhill soil.

## Deer Moss

Cold front, weather gray
and outlying jay call.
Sometimes mimics hawk.
Holds differently on
thinner, cooler air.

Saw clumps of deer moss
lining the barbed-wire fence.
In wiregrass land–uplands,
powdery lime and blue-green;
distinct in sandy spaces.

A closer look—skeletal
with branching arrays,
much like lightning strikes,
static and reaching
across quiet night skies.

Still and calm—here and now.
Holding to cold sandy patches
within the open spaces
in rusty oak leaf carpets,
amongst scrub oaks and blackjacks.

## Fox Squirrel

Fox squirrel, yellow tan,
standing tall in the path...
then bounding clumsily
through knee-high wiregrass,
and wildflowers—Blazing Star.
Set in the long shadows
of fall's afternoon sun.

He climbs as clumsily
as he runs—slow surge,
almost false effort to
act afraid, to get away.
Bunched on charred knot
where ancient branch
protruded from the old,
gnarled yellow pine.

## Gray Ghost

September and October
begins revolution...
Woods turned gray and old.

Out in the pines and bays
in murky hanging fog,
undergrowth, and canopy.

Where early morning stars
fade into false dawn...
Sit in wondering silence.

With pine bark and sap,
and sweet herbaceous smell
of the dying woods.

Hear early morning bird songs.
A drowsy nodding watcher
amongst the pines and bays...

With constant light rustle
in the leaf carpets below:
squirrel, bird, or more...

Eyes turned to see
twitch and shaking head,
the flicker of tail—twitch.

Moving like a ghost shadow,
here and gone...
Here and gone in shadows.

Hoof step and punch mark,
slowly, but deliberately,
sliding through palmettos.

Sliding out of view...
Flicker—white tail;
gray, brown winter coat.

Blink and gone,
fading and gone
Apparition—gray ghost.

## Cold November Morning

Cold weather,
front weather
in November.
All the Blackjacks
rusty—withering.
Sandy trails,
autumn trails
between the
dying grass.

Wouldn't you like
stand still
with hands in coat
and breathe it?
All the open spaces...
I dreamed of this.
Don't know when.
I dreamed of this.
Don't know where.

## Speckled Perch

Open waters,
deep and blue.
The sun begins
to rise with
rocking boat.

Rusty cypress
rings the lake
against fall
pastels, just
before the front.

On gentle
ripple wind
we make our
way to troll
deep depths.

Dark blue
and green
where schools
of silvery
fish suspend,

and drift
in water.
The bottom
descending,
rising again.

To see them
above in
magnificent,
spattered
speckles.

Silver to
black and
aqua greens,
and darkest
blue hues.

Tapestry of
deepest waters—
of worlds
below in sun's
fractured light.

# V

# Darkness Hangs in Winter Sky

## Walk to the Eagle's Nest

Walk to the eagle's nest,
around the ancient lakebed;
sunken gem set in the
sandy ridge, rolling hills,
as sea swells of wiregrass
and open pinelands shift.
Wet pines, dark lines in
the chop, chop expanse of
yellow-white winter grass.

I stop to watch
while white-tails scatter,
flagging flicker-tails bouncing,
their dark coats blending.
Pine needles cover sand trails
where the gopher tortoise
crossed in new spring green.
Not so long ago—yet far away.
No cactus bloom or Pawpaw.

Through remnant fall flowers,
like purple, blazing star....
These are the days we
dream of in the summer;
a cold sideways mist
and front clouds rushing,
while darkness setting in.

## Hunters in Winter Woods

Walk as shadows—early dawn,
darkness hangs in winter sky.
Drip-drop of last night's rain,
misstep popping—snapping twigs.
Settle, sit in leaf blankets,
fallen trees, and leafless vines;
waiting, hoping, cramped, and hungry.

Sit still! In whisper tone,
quick gray flash of phantoms—
winter ghost and flagging tail.
Never saw them... here they came...
as we sat inseparable to the ground.
As we blended in browns and grays,
And tried to be one with quiet forest.

Sitting, stalking, hunting—waiting
to kill in winter veiled woods...
I remember blood drops on yellow grass,
in woods where rotting logs lay crumbling.
Where mushrooms grow in small cities.
Where all is dying decay of winter forest,
amongst, leafless, reaching, skeleton trees.

## Ichetucknee in Winter

In blue, emerald green, reflecting the sun,
As currents flow and eelgrass sways,
Wandering waters spill into the run,
Through legions of cypress, bearded and
    gray.

And live oak branch, so crooked it hangs,
Slight touch of the water, the v-ripple flow.
Pools of azure where sun breaks the shade,
Near moss covered walls of ancient
    limestone.

Formations of fish, they slide, and they glide,
Or manatee slumbering alone in the bay.
The Kingfisher flying along as our guide,
As if he's our keeper, he shows us the way.

Impossible beauty, around every bend,
As heaven above was allowed to descend.

### "Bobwhite?"

They hurry, scurry across the sandy road,
to the blackberry briar thicket edge.

Where palmettos gently brush the ground...
speckled black, white–gold, and brown.

I heard his lonesome call "Bob-white?"
I've heard him at the edge of the scrub.

Firebird—flutter, flash between spaces,
in upland forest, in the 'crazy quilt' mosaic.

## Out in the Blackjacks

In December,
out in the Blackjacks,
there are sandy trails...
through parted seas
of rotted leaves.
All is pastel against
rusty, dead flags.
Corrosion fallen
from heavy summer.

In the Blackjacks
the afternoon is set,
light beryl, and luminous,
then resolved to gray.
On this day–crisp, cold;
flavor of ash and fire,
sounds ringing in echoed chambers...
Crunching, crackling, leaves;
an empty wooded cacophony.

Out in the Blackjack grove
where I once set my camp—
I burned an all-night fire.
I made many friends...
told stories in starry blue.
Felt, but didn't know it,
and made tableaus in the sun.

## Swindle Lake in Winter

Winter lake in cold, steel-blue
Sun reflects on windblown prairie
All is still, the quiet morning
Dawn prepares the coming day.

## Coots

In the bright
afternoon sun, I
saw little clumps

of black headed coots
with white billed,
bobbing heads.

Gray backs half
sunken like a ship
taking on water,

I hear their tired
whining—dipping,
dabbling in water.

Fly walking on water
with aqua blue
paddle feet. As if

unable to take off,
yet suddenly
here every year

when colder weather
returns. False duck,
loyal and unwavering.

## The Woods are Silent Now

Remember the deer running?
The way down to the creek?

I remember walking when
the moon was at its peak.

Laid down, became the dust,
the dust an empty street.

This place in all its mystery—
in the past where I retreat.

Black jacks and pine rows,
power lines and sand.

Arrowheads and rain wash,
lines that mark our hands.

Winter, winter, summer,
I bury in the ground.

Wander, wander, searching...
The woods are silent now.

## The North Fork

Many cold snags stand still
casting ripples on black water
with reflections, gray and blue.

All the while, sand rests in drifts
through Tag Alder thickets,
as if snow covered the ground.

Ushered along by the Kingfisher...
this black, tannic road cuts deep
into the interior; the hinterland.

Where old solemn cypress stand
guard and never change, with
wintery fingers reaching high.

## Black Creek Crayfish

Bounce along the shady stream,
up among the roots and rocks.
Spotted shoulder black and gold,
banded legs and rusty claw.

Minnows shudder floating by,
antenna out with beady eyes.
So many mysteries below,
so many worlds, the dark unknown.

## The Salt Marsh

In the backwater salt marsh flats,
the water birds step and dabble
near craggy mounds of mud covered
oyster beds, protruding into the air.

As tide moves in over the slick,
pockmarked sand, in murky blue
translucence... as Pelicans glide,
swoop, and dive, splashing valiantly.

The great white Egret struts so calm;
pure and proud, against the changing scene.

## One Trip Around the Sun

I'm back where I started...
one trip around the sun.
Standing in the river bottom—
All is gray and cold.

The swamp sits still
in black pool mirrors,
reflecting what I know now,
and not so much a year ago.

Yet the stone-colored trees
still reach for the sky.
Their trunks as marble
where all is dormant—resting.

In the cycles and seasons,
I have seen through the
woods and the water,
the wiregrass and moon.

And come to this journey's end,
yet never end forever.
For one journey leads to another,
just as death in winter
soon blooming lush and green.

# Acknowledgements

I'd like to thank everyone, past and present, that have encouraged my artistic endeavors, and especially those who have nurtured my interest in the Florida environment. Most of the poems in this collection were written in one calendar year. I focused my attention to wildlife, plants, and environments that I associate with each season, and tried to encapsulate my thoughts and feelings in connection with each. All the poems were written in Northeast and North-central Florida.

I would encourage you to visit some of the locations listed below. In these places, I found great inspiration for writing this book. I hope you will enjoy reading this collection as much as I enjoyed writing it.

*Mike Roess Gold Head Branch State Park*
*Anastasia State Park*
*Sweetwater Wetlands Park (Paynes Prairie)*
*North and South Fork of Black Creek*
*State Road 13 in Putnam and St. Johns County*
*Black Creek Ravines Conservation Area*
*Camp Blanding Wildlife Management Area*
*Santa Fe Swamp Conservation Area*
*Ichetucknee Springs State Park*
*Etoniah State Forest*
*Belmore State Forest*